W9-AKD-971

DATE DUE

JY 3 '89	SE 18 '91	JUN 27 '9
JY 11 '89	AP 30 '92	FEB 1 1 '9
AG 9 '89	MY 11 '92	JUN 2 4 '9
SE 5 '89	JY 27 '92	AUG 1 0 '9
SE 8 '89	MY 12 '93	JY 19 '0
SE 25 '89	OC 28 '93	JA 09 '02
OC 13 '89	JAN 27 '94	JY 01 '02
OC 27 '89	FEB 25 '94	AG 20 '0
NO 21 '89	MAR 31 '96	JY 3 '0
DE 7 '90	SEP 1 6 '9	JY 06 '0
JY 2 '91	OCT 31 '9	AG 03 '0
JY 30 '91	MAR 09 '9	OC 11 '1

$14.00
10.95

J

599.322   Green, Carl R
GRE   The rabbit

EAU CLAIRE DISTRICT LIBRARY

THE
RABBIT

BY
CARL R. GREEN
WILLIAM R. SANFORD

EDITED BY
JUDY LOCKWOOD

EAU CLAIRE DISTRICT LIBRARY

PUBLISHED BY
CRESTWOOD HOUSE
Mankato, MN, U.S.A.

80478

5/16/89 Childrens Press $14.00 10.95

LIBRARY OF CONGRESS CATALOGING IN PUBLICATION DATA

Green, Carl R.
  The rabbit

  (Wildlife, habits & habitat)
  Includes index.
  SUMMARY: Examines the physical characteristics, behavior, lifestyle, and natural environment of the rabbit and presents some advice about keeping this fast-breeding animal as a pet.
  1. Rabbits—Juvenile literature. 2. Cottontails—Juvenile literature. [1. Rabbits. 2. Cottontails] I. Sanford, William R. (William Reynolds), 1927-   . II. Lockwood, Judy. III. Title. IV. Series.
QL737.L32G74   1988   599.32'2—dc19   88-9601
ISBN 0-89686-387-5

International Standard Book Number:	Library of Congress Catalog Card Number:
0-89686-387-5	88-9601

PHOTO CREDITS:

Cover: DRK Photo: Leonard Lee Rue III
Tom Stack & Associates: (Susan Gibler) 8; (Robert C. Simpson) 11; (Alan D. Briere) 14; (W. Perry Conway) 17; (Rod Planck) 21, 24, 27; (John Shaw) 30; (Leonard Lee Rue III) 33; (C. Summers) 34; (Robert McKenzie) 39; (Gary Randall) 42; (Don & Ester Phillips) 44; (Jeff March) 4
DRK Photo: (Wayne Lankinen) 10; (Stephen J. Krasemann) 7, 12, 18, 23; (Tom A. Schneider) 37

Copyright© 1988 by Crestwood House, Inc. All rights reserved. No part of this book may be reproduced in any form without written permission from the publisher, except for brief passages included in a review. Printed in the United States of America.

Produced by Carnival Enterprises.

CRESTWOOD HOUSE

Box 3427, Mankato, MN, U.S.A. 56002

TABLE OF CONTENTS

The cottontail is the only wild rabbit in the United States.

INTRODUCTION:

Lauren led her American friend through the garden. Les was making his first trip to England, and she wanted to show him everything. They stopped when they came to the rabbit hutches.

"How many rabbits do you have?" Les wanted to know.

Lauren smiled. "In the spring, we'll have baby rabbits hopping all over the place," she said. "Right now, we just have two females and one big male. Duchess and Lady are the does. Duke is the buck. They're over here, in their cages. Don't you Americans keep rabbits?"

Les thought of his crowded California beach city and laughed. "I guess a few people keep rabbits as pets," he said. "Mostly, I see wild jackrabbits in the hills near my house."

Lauren fed a bit of clover to Duchess. "Lots of people make that mistake," she told Les. "Jackrabbits aren't rabbits at all, despite the name. People should call them 'jackhares,' because they're really hares. The only wild rabbits you have in the U.S. are the cottontails."

"I thought hare was just another name for rabbit," Les confessed. "What's the difference?"

"If you put a hare and a rabbit side by side," explained Lauren, "you'd see that they're not the same. For the most part, hares are bigger than rabbits. They have longer ears and legs, and their bodies aren't as chunky. Rabbits hop and scurry, but hares bound and leap—like those jackrabbits you saw."

"Is that all?" Les asked. He was letting Lady nibble on his fingertips. Her large, bright eyes looked soft and trusting.

"Well, baby rabbits are born without fur," Lauren went on. "They're almost completely helpless. Baby hares have a furry coat, and they can hop almost from the time they're born. Oh yes, there's one other thing. Rabbits and hares can't interbreed."

"You're quite an expert on rabbits," Les teased her.

"I have to be," Lauren said. "My parents won't let me keep animals if I don't study up on them. Someday I'd like to raise some hares, too."

"My third grade teacher used to raise hares," Les remembered. "He brought two of them to school during the science fair. They were Belgian hares, I think."

Lauren giggled. "Just when we had everything straight, you mention Belgian hares," she said. "Despite the name, what you saw were rabbits, not hares. The breed started in a part of Belgium called Flanders. My mother says they were bred from a very large rabbit called the Patagonian which is now extinct. Belgian hares were the first domestic rabbits

Hares have longer ears and legs than a rabbit.

imported into the United States. Because they're tall and lean, they do look like hares."

"Now I'm really mixed up," Les admitted.

"You're not the only one," Lauren assured him. "Rabbits and hares were once classed as rodents because their long front teeth never stop growing. That put them in the same family as rats and squirrels. Closer study, however, showed that rabbits have four upper front teeth to a rodent's two. Rabbits also have more cheek teeth, and they move their jaws differently."

The small, furry "rock rabbit" is a close cousin of rabbits and hares.

Lauren picked up Lady and pointed to her stumpy flag of a tail. "And rabbits and hares don't have long, rat-like tails. After looking at the differences, naturalists gave rabbits and hares their own order, the *lagomorpha.*"

"I have one more question," Les said. "Are all rabbits as fat and lazy as Lady?"

"Wild rabbits are fast and clever," Lauren said. "Just try to catch one! Their bodies are built for survival."

"I'd like to learn more about rabbits. Maybe I could raise them someday!" said Les.

CHAPTER ONE:

Rabbits have been domesticated for thousands of years. Large populations of wild rabbits, however, live wherever there is suitable habitat. They can be found on every continent and major island, except for Madagascar and Antarctica. They look a lot like domestic rabbits, but they are smarter, tougher, and quicker.

A growing family

All rabbits are plant-eating mammals that belong to the order lagomorpha. The lagomorphs are divided into two families. One family, the *ochotonidae*, is made up of furry, hamster-sized animals called "pikas." Some people call them "rock rabbits." The 44 species of rabbits and hares make up the second family, the *leporidae*.

The wild European rabbit has spread into many parts of the world. It is the ancestor of today's domestic rabbits. Thanks to careful breeding, domestic rabbits vary greatly in size, color, and length of fur. The American Rabbit Breeders Association registers 28 breeds, and at least 70 varieties.

In North and South America, the cottontail is the

native wild rabbit. Cottontails and wild European rabbits look very much alike. Let loose in the woods, however, a European rabbit would burrow into the earth, and a cottontail would nest above ground. Thirteen species of cottontails are found in North and South America. Typical are the eastern cottontail, the desert cottontail, and the swamp rabbit.

The eastern cottontail is one species of rabbit found in the U.S.

The desert cottontail makes its home in drier areas of the U.S.

Two lesser-known species are in danger of extinction. The volcano rabbit lives only on volcanic slopes near Mexico City. Farmers, hunters, and tourists have nearly destroyed its habitat. The Amami rabbit lives only on two small Japanese islands. Because of logging activities, the Amami rabbit population has shrunk to less than 5,000 animals.

The swamp rabbit, like other cottontails, nests above the ground.

Cat-sized and greyish-brown

Adult wild rabbits are cat-sized, weighing from two to four pounds (about 1 to 2 kilograms). By contrast, some domestic rabbits weigh up to 15 pounds (6.8 kg). Wild rabbits range in length from 13 to 17 inches (33 to 43 centimeters). The bucks are slightly larger than the does.

In the wild, a rabbit's fur is usually a speckled grey-brown that fades into a grey-white on the belly. The color helps the rabbit blend in with the grasses and leaves of its habitat. A few wild rabbits are born with white, black, and light tan coats. Domestic rabbits, by contrast, can be almost any color.

The rabbit's coat is made up of two types of hair. The long, coarse guard hairs stick out through the thick, wavy undercoat. It is the undercoat that gives rabbit fur its plush feeling. The coat protects the rabbit from heat, cold, and sun. It also provides a barrier against germs. Instead of sweating through its skin, the rabbit has a sweat gland under each forepaw.

Rabbits shed their fur once a year, a process known as molting. The molt starts in the early spring and lasts until fall. The new coat grows in thick and warm, just in time for winter's chilly winds. A female also sheds the fur from her belly when she's preparing to give birth. Lining the nest with hair makes it warm and soft

EAU CLAIRE DISTRICT LIBRARY

To blend in with its grassy surroundings, a wild rabbit's fur is often speckled with greys and browns.

for her litter. In addition, plucking the belly hair exposes the teats, so that the newborns can nurse.

Small heads and big teeth

A wild rabbit's head is a little under three inches (7 cm) long. The small nostrils are set in a patch of bare, moist skin. A rabbit's mouth seems quite large because of its small head. The top lip is divided, and pulls back to reveal the large front teeth. Long whiskers sprout from the areas around the eyes, cheeks, and mouth.

Six chisel-like cutting teeth (incisors) grow at the front of the rabbit's mouth. The upper jaw has four of the six incisors, with one pair growing behind the other. The incisors grow throughout the rabbit's life. Constant chewing on tough, woody branches keeps them worn down. A toothless gap exists between the incisors and the cheek teeth. The rabbit can pinch in the skin on each side of the gap, thus screening out unwanted dirt or bits of wood. The rabbit's 22 cheek teeth (molars) grow behind the gap. The cheek teeth grind the food to a pulp before the rabbit swallows.

Keen senses keep the rabbit alive

A wild rabbit needs keen eyes, ears, and nose if it is to stay alive. Large eyes set on the sides of the head allow it to see in all directions. Vision overlaps in front and in back, so that nothing escapes the rabbit's notice. Because danger is greatest at night when the rabbit is feeding, it also has excellent night vision. In addition to the usual upper and lower eyelids, rabbits have a third eyelid. This extra eyelid can be closed to protect the eye during fights or dust storms. Long eyelashes add additional protection.

A rabbit's ears are one of its most notable features. Long and sensitive, they pick up the slightest sound. A rabbit holds its ears upright, except when it's frightened or when it's running. At those times, the ears lay back against its body. Each ear turns in any direction, so the rabbit can "tune in" on sounds from any angle. The ears also help regulate the rabbit's body temperature. When blood pumps through the ears in hot weather, excess heat is given off. This lowers the body temperature. In cold weather, the rabbit conserves its body heat by cutting down the flow of blood through the ears.

Finally, rabbits have a keen sense of smell and touch. The rabbit constantly twitches its nose and sniffs the air. As the nostrils open, they expose two special pads that react to the slightest of odors. Thus, the faint scent of a distant predator is enough to send the rabbit hopping to safety. Long, sensitive whiskers grow around the rabbit's mouth. The whiskers serve as "feelers" to guide the rabbit through dark, underground tunnels.

A hopper, not a walker

Rabbits don't walk, they hop. The reason is easy to see. The hind legs are much longer than the front legs. When frightened, the rabbit pushes off with its

When a rabbit is frightened, its ears lay back against its body.

powerful hind legs. It lands on its front paws, and pushes off again with its hind legs. The process sounds awkward, but wild rabbits have been timed at speeds of 15 miles (24 kilometers) per hour. A running rabbit can change directions instantly, without slowing down.

The front paws have five toes, and the hind paws have four toes. Each toe has a sharp, strong claw, and each paw is covered with hair. The hair gives the rabbit a non-slip tread on icy hillsides. When a rabbit sits up on its hind legs, it is usually looking, listening,

17

A desert cottontail listens carefully for predators before entering a nearby bush.

or sniffing for danger. A rabbit also can balance on its rear paws to reach for food that's above its head.

A fast heart rate

Strangely enough, domesticated rabbits do not have strong hearts. Pet rabbits sometimes die of heart failure caused by a bad fright. Wild rabbits could not survive with that handicap. At any moment, they may have to make a quick, darting run to a hiding place. The rabbit's heart beats 200 times a minute, almost three times faster than the human heart. This rapid heartbeat pumps oxygen-rich blood to all parts of the body. Their habitat is full of danger, but wild rabbits are well equipped to survive.

CHAPTER TWO:

Wild rabbits have adapted to habitats all around the globe. They can survive desert heat and near-Arctic cold. Their favorite habitat, however, is one with light, sandy soil and plenty of grass, bushes, and trees. An English woodland or the overgrown borders of a Missouri dairy farm would be ideal. Long winters, heavy rains, and high altitudes are not to their liking.

The wild European rabbit first appeared in the northwest corner of Africa, Spain, and Portugal. In time, the rabbit might have spread across Europe and Africa all by itself. Humans, however, helped it along. Wherever armies marched and navies sailed, they took rabbits along for food. When some of the rabbits escaped along the way, they started new populations. Thus, despite its name, the European rabbit can be found in Asia, Australia, and many other faraway places.

Home is a network of tunnels

The European rabbit is the only rabbit that lives in underground burrows. The burrows, also known as warrens, are made up of a network of tunnels. The female rabbits do most of the tunneling. They dig with their front legs and push the dirt out behind with their hind legs. Each tunnel averages about six inches (15 cm) in width. Some tunnels slant downward to a depth of ten feet (3 meters). Rabbits usually dig their warrens on sloping ground. This allows ground water to run off and keeps the tunnels dry.

A typical warren has several entrances and exits. The entrance holes lead to tunnels that branch off in many directions. The tunnels lead to larger "rooms" known as stops. Each stop is home to a rabbit. The females dig a separate nesting stop for their young. In addition to the main tunnels, the rabbits dig smaller tunnels called bolt holes. The bolt holes serve as escape routes if a weasel or other predator invades the warren.

A warren grows and grows

European rabbits remain underground for much of the day, but leave the warren at night to feed. They fill the daylight hours by sleeping, digesting their food, and caring for their young. In good weather, they may come out to lie in the sun. As the population grows, new tunnels add to the size of the warren. After several years, a large warren may provide stops for several hundred rabbits.

Mounds of dirt mark the entrance to a rabbit's warren.

The feeding territory around a warren extends as much as 600 yards (550 m) in any direction. This takes in an area of about 50 acres (20 hectares). If food is plentiful, the rabbits stay closer to the warren. The entrances are marked by mounds of dirt pushed out from the tunnels. The rabbits also leave their tracks, bits of fur, and piles of droppings nearby.

Bucks rule the warren

Hundreds of rabbits may live in a warren, but each rabbit belongs to a smaller "family." Families are made up of an older buck, several does, and their young. The buck marks his territory by leaving droppings along its borders. He also scent-marks rocks and plants, using the smelly fluid from a gland under his chin. If an outsider tries to steal one of his does, the buck fights back. He will also try to guard his family from a predator. An angry buck has been known to drive off a skunk with slashing kicks from his hind legs.

Because each buck keeps several does, only the strongest bucks can win mates. In a fight for a doe, the bucks kick, bite, and scratch. Injuries suffered in these fights can be fatal. Most fights, however, end with the loser running away or lying down to signal defeat. Timid bucks often go off and live by themselves. Unable to join a family, they nest in piles of rock, under fallen trees, or in thick underbrush.

A strict diet of "green stuff"

Rabbits are herbivores, animals that live almost entirely on plants. Their diet is mostly grass,

One of the desert cottontail's favorite meals is wildflowers.

wildflowers, clover, leaves, and tender twigs. Once in a while, a rabbit will eat snails or earthworms. An adult rabbit eats about one pound (0.4 kg) of food each day. That's equal to about one-fourth of its body weight! When it's thirsty, a rabbit will drink from ponds, streams, waterholes, or puddles. Much of their water, however, comes from the plants they eat.

If rabbits ate only wild plants, farmers might let them live in peace. Rabbits pass up tough, prickly weeds, however, to munch on lettuce, beans, wheat, carrots, and other farm crops. Left alone in a pasture, rabbits also eat the grasses farmers need for their cattle and other grazing animals. In snowy climates, rabbits do a different kind of damage. Unable to find their usual food, they kill young trees by stripping the bark from the trunks.

Rabbits groom themselves to keep their fur clean and to get rid of small insects.

Quick to feed, slow to digest

Rabbits feed almost entirely at night. They eat quickly, always alert for danger. By first light, they're safely back in their hiding places, ready to rest and digest their diet of plant food. Digesting what they've eaten is a two-step process. After chewing and swallowing the food once, rabbits must digest it a second time. They do this by eating their own first droppings as soon as they pass them. These soft, round pellets of half-digested food are rich in protein.

While digestion goes on, the rabbit rests and grooms itself. Grooming is the process of cleaning the fur. After licking those places it can reach with its tongue, the rabbit spreads saliva on its front paws. Then it uses its paws like a wash cloth to scrub its head and long ears. When it's time to pass the hard, dry second droppings, the rabbit goes out to the same "toilet" everytime. It never soils its own nest.

A favorite of predators

Rabbits make very few sounds. To warn other rabbits of danger, they thump the ground with their hind feet. The sight of a rabbit sitting up or hopping quickly away also alerts other rabbits. Aside from a few low growls and grunts, the rabbit's only sound is the terrorized scream it makes when it's cornered. The scream sometimes startles a predator and gives the rabbit a chance to escape.

Many predators hunt the rabbit. The list includes dogs, cats, weasels, badgers, coyotes, wolves, foxes, snakes, eagles, hawks, and owls. Young rabbits are in the greatest danger. Predators catch them before they've learned how to run and hide. In one study, naturalists followed 280 young rabbits that were born during a single spring and summer. By fall, 252 of them were dead. Many were killed by predators, but others died of hunger, disease, or drowning.

In captivity, a rabbit may live up to ten years. In the wild, only a few rabbits live that long. The average life span of wild rabbits is probably closer to 18 months. Even so, most rabbits complete a full life cycle in that brief time.

CHAPTER THREE:

Only the hum of insects and the faint rustle of a summer breeze break the quiet. The Kansas woodland lies dreaming under a deep blue sky. A small doe is nesting in the tangled shadow of a blackberry thicket.

Lapi's brown fur, speckled with black, blends with the grass and leaves. Small bunches of brown hair

Wild rabbits usually live about 18 months.

stick to the bush above her. Lapi is going through her spring molt. When she twists to groom her hind legs, the patch of white on the underside of her tail shows. This is the fluff of "cotton" that gives her species its name. Content now, she closes her eyes and sleeps. Inside her body, five tiny cottontails wait to be born.

Birth of a litter

That night, Lapi hops to a protected spot next to a rotting fence post. Instinct tells her that her litter will be born that night. She scoops out a nest hole that's a little bigger than her own body. The nest is about six inches (15 cm) deep. After she finishes digging, Lapi lines the nest with leaves and bits of fur. Then she crouches down and waits.

The big buck who fathered Lapi's new litter is nowhere to be seen. Lapi drove him away after they mated four weeks ago. The bucks will kill newborn kittens, as the young are called, if the females let them get too close. This will be Lapi's third litter of the season. Most litters have eight kittens or less, but Lapi's second litter was huge. Just six weeks ago, she gave birth to 14 kittens!

Lapi's five kittens are born just before dawn. The tiny creatures are blind and deaf, barely strong enough to squirm. Their dark skin is bare, with faint brown markings. The largest kitten weighs only two ounces (57 grams). Lapi lies beside them and lets them nurse from her teats. When the kittens are full, she covers them with a blanket of fur, leaves, and twigs. The cover keeps the litter warm and hides them from predators.

Danger is always close by

Lapi hops away to find food for herself. The kittens are helpless, and many predators live in the woods. After eating her fill, Lapi hollows out her own sleeping spot not far from the nest. Naturalists speak of these small ovals as "forms." Lapi licks up the dew that gathers on the grass. It's enough to take care of her thirst.

Almost at once, a red fox walks into the clearing. Hunting has been poor, and the fox is hungry. Lapi knows only one way to save her kittens. Just as the fox nears the nest, she jumps up as if she's been startled. The fox sees the sudden movement and springs after the doe. White cottontail flashing, Lapi leads him in a mad dash through the woods. Far from the nest, she ducks into a hole under a dead tree. The fox digs into the twisted roots for a few minutes, but he can't reach his prey. Finally, he gives up and trots off to find an easier breakfast.

Lapi returns to the nest after the sun goes down. She

Young eastern cottontails can stand upright ten days after birth.

uncovers the kittens and feeds them. Then she licks them clean with her tongue. The doe returns to feed the kittens several times during the night. The night feedings must last them during the daylight hours while she is away from the nest.

Growing fast

Four days later, the kittens have grown a coat of soft fur. Their eyes begin to open at the end of the sixth day. The little ones are stronger now. They wiggle and push against each other. When it rains at night, they huddle together in the warm nest. One of the does has never been as strong as her nestmates. She gets crowded out at feeding time and grows weaker. A few days later she dies. Lapi drags the little body away from the nest.

Ten days after birth, the kittens' ears are open and standing upright. The sounds of the woods are new, and some are frightening. The kittens freeze when they hear the deep voice of an owl or the soft footsteps of a skunk. Instinct tells them to stay quiet. An hour later, they hear Lapi's familiar hop-hop-hop. The four kittens tumble out of the nest and scurry to meet her.

The kittens are now too big for the nest. Lapi has stopped trying to repair it each night. Her milk is drying up, and she can no longer satisfy the kittens' hunger. They begin to nibble on the dried grass that lines the nest. When that's gone, they creep out to try the tender plants that grow nearby. After eating, they huddle together for warmth and security.

Playing and learning

In their third week, the young rabbits play active games. One game looks like hide-and-seek and tag all in one. They dart back and forth, agile and quick. In the next instant, they duck under a bush and freeze. Only their bright eyes and twitching noses give away their hiding places. The games have a serious purpose.

A rabbit's safety depends on its ability to outrun predators and to hide from danger. Lapi's kittens are learning these important lessons.

During the day, the young rabbits sleep in forms they make in the tall grass. At this age, they make their forms close to each other. When they go out to find food at night, they head off in different directions.

At four weeks, the young cottontails are half grown. Lapi has left them to mate again. Each night, the young ones go farther and farther to find food. The buck is the bravest. He's discovered the garden next to a nearby farmhouse.

The buck's dinners of cabbages and turnips almost end in tragedy a week later. Just as he enters the garden, a dog runs at him from behind a shed. The buck leaps back, spins, and darts for the woods. The dog bounds after him, teeth snapping. Just in time, the small rabbit slips under a fence, leaving the angry dog behind. After that, the buck stays away from the garden.

End of the summer

The first frosts send a chill through the woods. The three-month-old rabbits are fully grown. They've grown their thick coat of adult fur and put on a layer of fat. They'll need both during the coming winter.

By the time they're three weeks old, young rabbits venture out of their nest and explore their surroundings.

The does born early in the spring have already mated, but the last does born that season won't mate until the spring. Each young rabbit finds a winter form of its own, away from the others.

Food is hard to find during the cold, snowy days that follow. The rabbits eat twigs, dead grass, and gnaw at the bark of small trees. One doe finds her way into a barn. The horses scare her, but she stays because the barn is warm and full of hay.

When spring returns, the does pair off with the bucks who come to court them. Each pair plays and

To keep warm during the winter months, rabbits find shelter anywhere they can.

feeds together before they mate. Four weeks later, the does will be ready to give birth. They chase the bucks away and build their nests. A new cycle in the life of cottontail rabbits is beginning.

34

CHAPTER FOUR:

Humans and rabbits have shared the woods and fields of the earth since the earliest times. Twenty thousand years ago, Stone Age people painted colorful pictures of rabbits on the walls of their caves. Records show that the ancient Egyptians hunted rabbits for food and sport, as did other early peoples.

Rabbits inspire many beliefs

At the same time, rabbits played a role in early religions. Some of the beliefs were based on the speed with which rabbits breed. When the Chinese sacrificed rabbits to their gods, they prayed that their crops would be as fruitful as the rabbits. Historians say that the legend of the Easter bunny started about the same time. The modern story began with a fable about a rabbit that lays a nestful of colored eggs every spring.

In the Middle Ages, people believed that rabbits could keep them safe from witches. In England, men and women wore the left hind foot of a rabbit around their necks. The charm was supposed to guard them from evil spirits. Today, that belief continues with the "lucky" rabbit's foot that some people carry on key chains.

Rabbits go to work

The Romans were probably the first civilization to use rabbits as domestic animals. Roman soldiers carried crates of rabbits with them on long marches. The rabbits were part of their food supply. When they camped, the soldiers turned the rabbits loose to graze behind stone walls. Some of these rabbits escaped. They became part of the wild animal population wherever the Romans traveled.

By the 1300s, Europeans were breeding rabbits for size and color. In each litter, they selected the biggest and most colorful kittens. By mating these hand-picked rabbits, they developed dozens of domestic breeds. Because they were cheap and easy to raise, rabbits became a favorite food. People who eat rabbit today say it is mild-tasting, somewhat like chicken. Rabbit meat is also low in fat.

Rabbit fur has been made into winter coats for thousands of years. Many people, however, refused to buy a rabbit fur coat because it's one of the cheaper furs. As a result, furriers learned long ago to dye the fur to look like expensive sable or mink. Long-haired rabbits also grow a fine wool for sweaters and mittens. An Angora rabbit can produce up to a pound (0.4 kg) of wool a year.

Rabbits multiply beyond reason

Starting in the 1400s, Europeans took rabbits with them when they went exploring. In 1418, the Portuguese set rabbits free on the island of Porto Santo in the Atlantic Ocean. The island didn't have any natural predators to control the fast-breeding rabbits. Unable to protect their crops, the people who lived there were forced to leave.

The pattern was repeated in Australia. In 1859, a settler brought two dozen wild European rabbits from

People used to believe that rabbits could keep witches away.

England. He thought the rabbits would be a good addition to the wild game of the continent. Turned loose in the province of Victoria, the rabbits bred freely. Within 20 years, the first 24 had multiplied into millions of rabbits! In self defense, Australians built a 2,000-mile (3,200-km) rabbit fence to protect their grasslands. They tried poison, traps, and guns, but nothing could control the hungry rabbits.

In the 1950s, the government introduced a deadly rabbit disease called myxomatosis (pronounced mik-so-muh-TOE-sus). Spread by fleas and mosquitos, the virus disease kills only European rabbits. It seldom affects cottontails or hares. After infected rabbits were turned loose in the countryside, millions of wild rabbits died. With the rabbit population under control, the grasslands became green again.

Myxomatosis in France and England

Landowners in France also were being overrun by rabbits. In 1952, a Frenchman introduced myxomatosis on his estate. Within months, over 35 percent of the domestic and wild rabbits of France were dead. The disease crossed the English Channel to the British Isles the next year. Farmers rejoiced as the rabbit population fell to one-tenth its former level.

In 1859 there were so many rabbits in Australia that a 2,000-mile rabbit fence was built to protect the grasslands!

The loss of rabbits led to unexpected results. First, the number of predators dropped. There were fewer foxes, weasels, hawks, and other meat-eaters. Country lanes became choked with long grasses, brambles, and young trees. The edges of plowed fields turned into tangles of weeds and wildflowers bloomed everywhere. One report stated that the countryside looked as it did in 1840. That was a time when wild rabbits were scarce.

Always popular with children

Farmers may not care for rabbits, but children love them. Stuffed toy rabbits and bunny slippers are always popular. Children's stories often feature rabbits. Beatrix Potter created the famous Peter Rabbit, who raids Farmer McGregor's cabbage patch. In the Uncle Remus stories, Br'er Rabbit outsmarts Br'er Fox and his other animal neighbors. Today's Saturday morning cartoons wouldn't be the same without that "wascally wabbit," Bugs Bunny.

Rabbits make good pets. Caring for a rabbit is different than caring for a dog or cat, however. Anyone who wants to keep rabbits should be aware of their special needs.

CHAPTER FIVE:

The sight of a baby rabbit makes people want to hold it, pet it, and take it home. The rabbits sold in pet stores have all been bred and raised in captivity. These rabbits like people and make loving pets. Wild rabbits are another matter, because they can never be completely tamed. They're much better off in the wild.

Choosing a rabbit

Most people think of pet rabbits as furry white animals with pink eyes. These "Easter rabbits" are only one of many varieties from which to choose. You can buy a tiny Netherland dwarf or a much larger Flemish giant. You can pick a short-haired argente bleu or a long-haired Angora. Rabbits come in lovely shades of brown, tan, grey, grey-blue, black, and cream. Most have solid colors, but some have handsome spots. You can even buy a French lop, with ears that droop almost to the ground.

Whatever breed you pick, look for a plump, furry rabbit with bright, clear eyes. Its ears should stand straight up (unless it's a lop). Watch out for a runny nose; it's a sign of illness. You can choose either a buck or a doe, as both make good pets. Your rabbit should be at least two months old. Younger rabbits may have been weaned, but they're not ready to leave their mothers.

Housing a pet rabbit

You can raise a pet rabbit indoors or outdoors. A single rabbit, kept in a small indoor hutch, can be

Today, pet rabbits come in many sizes and colors.

given the run of the house. Paper-train your rabbit the same way you would train a puppy. Remember that rabbits always use the same spot for their toilet. Your job is to get your pet started in the right place.

A rabbit hutch should be at least four feet long, two feet wide, and two feet high (1.2 x 0.6 x 0.6 m). A hutch this large gives the rabbit space for exercise. Cover one end of the hutch so that the rabbit has a private area for sleeping. The roof should come off for easy cleaning. If you're using the hutch outdoors, it should be kept off the ground. Make it with a waterproof roof and side flaps that can be closed during cold or wet weather. Rabbits quickly learn to drink from water bottles that hang on the side of the hutch.

Care and feeding

Like all pets, rabbits need a lot of care. Their "toilet" should be cleaned every day and the water should be changed. Wood shavings or hay make good bedding materials, but they must be changed once a week. Remove any uneaten food from the hutch. Spoiled food may make your rabbit sick. Keep twigs in the hutch for the rabbit to chew. This will keep its teeth worn down.

Feed your rabbit twice a day. This can be tricky, because rabbits will overeat if you let them. Pet stores sell a special rabbit food that provides a balanced diet.

A mother and her "kitten" cuddle together for protection and warmth.

Many rabbit owners feed these pellets to their pets in the morning, followed by a dinner of vegetables or greens in the evening. Rabbits love lettuce, pea pods, spinach, carrots, apples, corn, and oats. You can also feed grass and tender green shoots from the yard. Finally, give them the rock salt and vitamins they need in order to stay healthy.

Raising your own rabbits

Many rabbit owners enjoy the task of raising their own rabbits. If you want to do this, wait until the does are eight months old before breeding them for the first time. If you don't have a buck, ask a local rabbit owner for help. After she's mated, give your doe a nesting box inside her hutch. The doe will line the box with bits of straw and fur from her own body. Feed her extra grain and bread soaked in milk.

The kittens will be born in about four weeks. Don't touch them for at least five days. If you handle the kittens too soon, the doe may abandon them. Her milk will nourish them for the first few weeks. After that, the fast-growing kittens will nibble on grass and garden vegetables. After two months, add vitamins to their diet to prevent a disease called rickets.

What can I do with all these rabbits?

What will you do, now that you have a litter of active, healthy rabbits on your hands? Remember, in a single season, one doe can provide you with 30 or more young! You can give a few away to friends, but what about the rest? Pet stores will buy healthy young rabbits, but they prefer the special breeds. Children who live on farms would suggest another use for rabbits: you can sell your surplus stock to be used as food.

Talk this matter over with your parents before breeding your doe. Keeping a pet rabbit is a lot of fun, but it's also a big responsibility.

MAP:

Most cottontail rabbits live within these areas.

Most European rabbits live within these areas.

INDEX/GLOSSARY

WILDLIFE
HABITS & HABITAT

READ AND ENJOY THE SERIES:

If you would like to know more about all kinds of wildlife, you should take a look at the other books in this series.

You'll find books on bald eagles and other birds. Books on alligators and other reptiles. There are books about deer and other big-game animals. And there are books about sharks and other creatures that live in the ocean.

In all of the books you will learn that life in the wild is not easy. But you will also learn what people can do to help wildlife survive. So read on!

EAU CLAIRE DISTRICT LIBRARY